PUNCILITIS
And Other Diseases
Curable, of course, by Punicillin

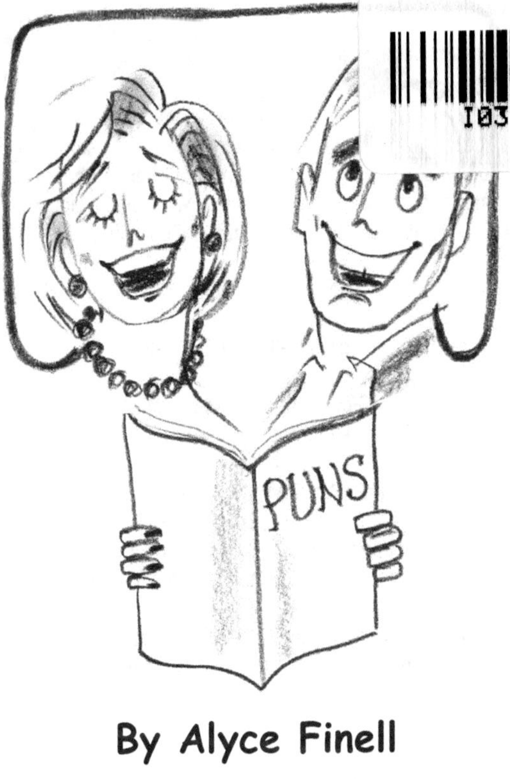

By Alyce Finell
Illustrations by Ed Kurtzman

The Three Tomatoes Book Publishing

Copyright © 2021 by Alyce Finell

All rights reserved. No part of this book may be reproduced in any form or by any electronic or mechanical means including information storage and retrieval systems, without permission in writing from the publisher. The only exception is by a reviewer, who may quote short excerpts in a review. For permission requests, please address The Three Tomatoes Publishing.

Published October 2021

ISBN: 978-1-7376177-2-3

For information address:
The Three Tomatoes Book Publishing
6 Soundview Rd.
Glen Cove, NY 11542

Cover and Interior Illustrations: Ed Kurtzman
Cover and interior design: Susan Herbst

All company and/or product names may be trade names, logos, trademarks, and/or registered trademarks are the property of their respective owners.

Introduction

I'm not sure how punny this book will be, but I'm going to sharpen my puncil for it...

If I'm punctual, this may be published; if not, this will merely be a sweet and pungent experience for all.

Perhaps it should begin with the famous words "Once upun a time..."

Whatever it is, it is a collection of odds and ends, random thoughts, and repartee, dedicated to my dear friends and relatives who moan and groan in happiness as they urge me to puntificate!

Some psychics work only as the spirit moves them...

Puncilitis and Other Diseases 1

I know a horticulturist who's a blooming idiot...

**How come a fireplace remains healthy,
even with the flu?**

The tennis pro who overcharges has some racket...

If you associate with an optometrist,
it's possible you'll be framed...

A boxer in training leads a spartan life...

Have you ever met a dentist who wasn't down in the mouth?

Then there was the law student who insisted on reading Playboy magazine - it was a case of tit for tort!

When you hurt your thumb, it's really thumb-thing!

I know one love affair that didn't work out because it was a case of bed and bored!

**One lamp to another: So watt's new?
I'm working on a shadey deal!**

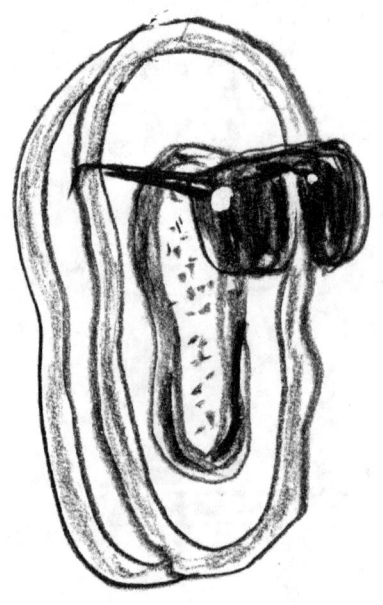 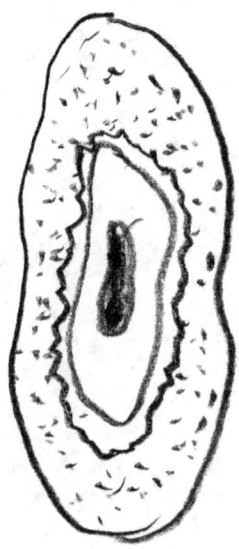

**One cell annoyed by another cell:
"Stop it – I vant to be a clone!"**

A novice milking a cow can cause udder distress...

Totally annoyed with a client who was questioning a window treatment, the interior decorator said "It's curtains for them!"

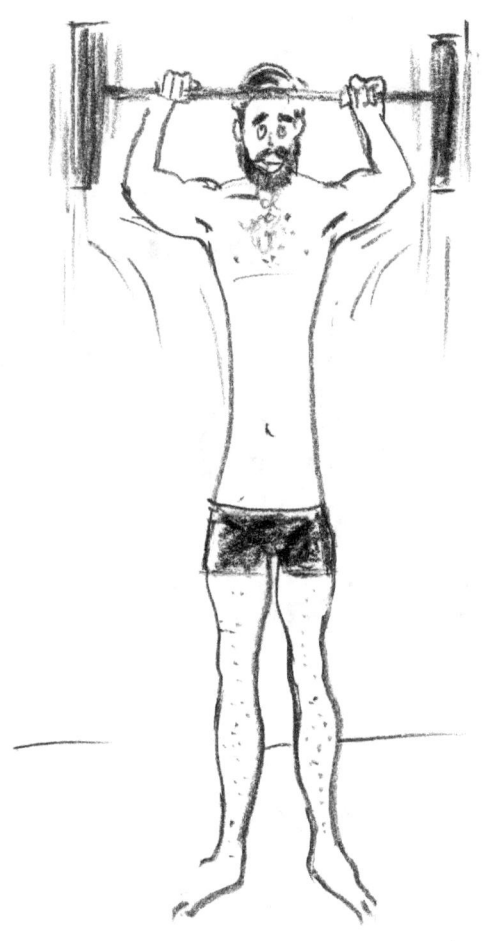

An exercise teacher is always stretching the point...

Baseball players tend to be a little batty...

A waiter has to traypse from one table to another...

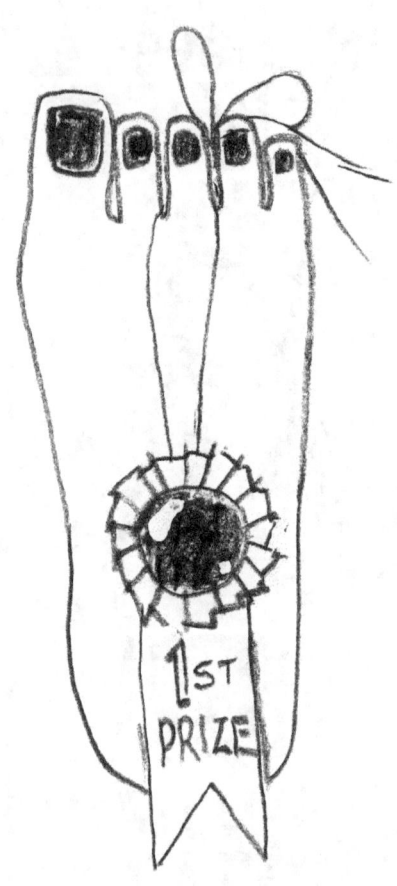

The podiatrist said his patient's recovery was a toe-tal success...

Be careful your masseuse doesn't rub you the wrong way!

The girl who wants to marry the carpenter said she's going to nail him!

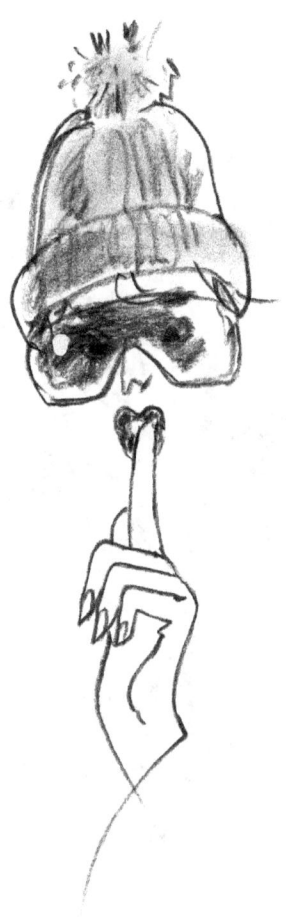

**Skiers seem to prefer peace and quiet -
they're always schussing...**

A pianist knows 88 keys to happiness...

An artist I know decided to give his girlfriend the brush off - found her less than palletable...

Most members of nudist colonies are barely there...

Training wild animals is a beastly business.

One mother had so many clothes to iron, it became a pressing problem.

I met a fabric designer who's very chintzy.

The photographer, annoyed with his model, told his assistant to shutter up!

One man's pipe dream is to carve corn cobs.

**Fishermen always have reely good times —
especially if they cast no aspersions!**

My friend Elza decided to take a course in aroma therapy. It must have been scent-sational!

Would a person who latch hooks rugs be a hooker?

It's easy to pine in the forest.

The other day my chiropractor cracked me up.

Can you imagine — a milliner capsizes all day!

A stockbroker bought a three piece suit so he would have a vested interest.

A man, annoyed by the click, click click of his wife's knitting, said "Please, stop needling me!"

When it came time for trial between the tailor and the men's haberdashery, the judge announced that they would now open the suitcase...

**A woman misplaced her handbag -
was told to pursue it!**

Years ago the news that electricity had been discovered was, indeed, shocking!

The auto mechnic decided to take a brake
for lunch...

The audience of an over zealous actor lecturing about humor ended up with ham on wry...

The judge was looking for a secretary justice type!

A carpet salesman should be very rugged...

A man who wears a toupee has a hair raising experience every day...

A tree surgeon went out on a limb, undoubtedly because he decided to branch out...

Of all the sections in an orchestra, the violinists are most high strung...

A frustrated singer I know opened a shoe store —
the only way he was able to get into shoe biz ...
Of course, that's better than being a loafer.
He succeeded because he was a good sole, even
though his wife accused him of being a heel.
She constantly laced him out. Sometimes he'd stick
out his tongue and slipper a flat insult just to pump
up his ego - then he'd sneaker a kiss to apologize.
They shoe-nuff had some crazy relationship!

Quiz: How many puns can you find?

A psychologist, upon listening to one more nightmare, was not convinced that his was a dream job.

This book should be up for capital punishment!

Special Thanks

Randie Levine-Miller
Cheryl Benton
Ed Kurtzman
Ruth Kurtzman
Julie Kurzman
Ken August (great punster)
Rick Perkal (great punster)
Iris Hinden (great sister)
Sharon & Ron Kahn
Kathleen Perkal
Joy Perkal
Marianne Friedman
Barbara & George Davidson
Dr. Albert Ross
Willie Mae Perry
Rhonda & Anthony Cutler
John Tantullo (great punster)
Alan Eichler
Jim & AJ Jimirro
Lydia Wilen
Alix Cohen
Sidney Myer
Carole Potter
Norma Frampton
Iris Williams
Tory Fretz
Bill Lanese
Mom & Dad

ABOUT THE AUTHOR

Alyce Finell is an Emmy® and Ace award-winning TV producer and writer who's held major network TV executive positions. She was responsible for the development and production of more than 40 TV series. The recipient of the 2016 Ruth Kurtzman Lifetime Achievement Award from Cabaret Cares. she serves as president of Finell Enterprises which includes diverse activities in PR and related fields, as well as her own jewelry designs. She is especially proud of helping to create the Mabel Mercer Foundation now in its third decade of keeping alive the Great American Songbook. To showcase her passion for lyrical, singable melody, she has created a musical fantasy titled "Mabel's Place," her own love song to the cabaret community. It has been described as "*American Idol* meets *The Fantasticks* and *Ed Sullivan!*" Seeking a producer.

ABOUT THE ILLUSTRATOR

A graduate of the Philadelphia Museum College of Art, **Ed Kurtzman** established himself in New York as one of the country's foremost fashion illustrators. His work has been featured in ads for many luxury retail stores, national magazines, and Vogue Patterns. Ed is the recipient of two Art Director's Awards and Fashion Ad of the Year for retail ads in *The New York Times*. Ed is also a portrait and fine artist, as well as a graphic designer, and his artwork and drawings are included in private collections in the US and abroad. NBC and *The New York Times* have both done stories on Ed's illustrations. As a member of AFTRA and SAG, Ed has acted in film and television commercials for a wide range of products and services.

www.ingramcontent.com/pod-product-compliance
Lightning Source LLC
Chambersburg PA
CBHW062202100526
44589CB00014B/1920